(F) IN EXAMS

JOKE BOOK

F IN EXAMS JOKE BOOK

With thanks to Lauren Housden

Summersdale Publishers Ltd
46 West Street
Chichester
West Sussex
PO19 1RP
UK

www.summersdale.com

Printed and bound by CPI Group (UK) Ltd, Croydon, CR0 4YY

ISBN: 978-1-84953-775-9

Substantial discounts on bulk quantities of Summersdale books are available to corporations, professional associations and other organisations. For details contact Nicky Douglas by telephone: +44 (0) 1243 756902, fax: +44 (0) 1243 786300 or email: nicky@summersdale.com.

F IN EXAMS JOKE BOOK

THE BEST (AND WORST) JOKES AND TEST PAPER BLUNDERS

Richard Benson

summersdale

Also in this Series

Contents

Introduction

F in Exams is back! It's time to relive those scary school exam papers once more. This most recent harvest of hilariously wrong answers to real exam questions certainly won't have earned an A★, more like an E for effort.

The laughs don't stop there, with some of the best (and naffest) jokes from the school playground, which are guaranteed to tickle your funny bone.

Going back to school has never been so funny!

Richard Benson

Physics

How does an earth wire protect the user of an electrical appliance?

It's packed full of earth so no electricity can pass through it.

Why are earth wires used in electrical appliances?

Because we're trying to be eco-friendly and use nature's resources.

What do you call bad-tempered bacteria?

A cross culture.

Give one reason why copper is used on the base of saucepans.

It looks nice when they're hanging up.

Physics

A stretched rubber band is an example of elastic potential energy. Name one other example.

My stretchy waistband after Sunday dinner.

What did the cross-eyed teacher say to the head teacher?

I can't control my pupils!

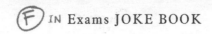

Explain the word inertia.

Opposite of auterxtia

What force draws objects away from the centre of rotation?

The Force (dark side).

Explain the term 'quantum entanglement'.

A complicated mess.

Physics

Why can dogs hear sounds that we can't?

We don't know what sounds they hear because we can't hear them?

It's said that all the matter that makes up the human race could fit in a sugar cube. Why is this?

Everyone loves sugar - it's all that matters.

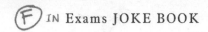

Why did the cell cross the microscope?

To get to the other side.

What is the hardest natural material known to man?

Rocks.

Give one reason why scientists think the universe is expanding.

Every time they measure it the length changes.

What is the first law of thermodynamics?

Don't tuck your shirt into your long johns, Granddad.

Explain the difference between a direct current (DC) and alternating current (AC).

D and A.

What is the difference between ammonia and pneumonia?

Ammonia comes in bottles, pneumonia comes in chests.

What is a supernova?

It's what posh people say when they're pleased.

Some roller coasters can produce a G-force of 4–6 kg. What is G-force and how does it affect the human body?

G-force comes from G-strings when they are too tight, especially in the bottom area.

Which classic adventure novel follows the tale of a group of rabbits as they escape the destruction of their warren and seek a new home?

Peter Rabbit

The following poem is an example of which form of Japanese poetry?

'The moment two bubbles
are united, they both vanish.
A lotus blooms.'

Manga.

Name two reasons to be a teacher.

July and August.

What is the main theme in *Of Mice and Men*?

Rodents and humans.

What kind of birds do you find in captivity?

Jailbirds.

Give one example of a 'crossover' novel.

Twilight.

What are adjectives?

Jectives that have been added on.

Which American novelist is famous for writing the Pulitzer Prize-winning *To Kill A Mockingbird*?

Lee Harper

What makes Atticus Finch such a memorable character in *To Kill A Mockingbird*?

His unusual name.

What is the difference between a colon and a semicolon?

These are also known as the large intestine and the small intestine.
The difference is mainly size.

Write a sentence which includes an oxymoron.

My friend Sam is big, tall and silly; he's a bit of an oxymoron.

William Wordsworth's famous poem 'I Wandered Lonely as a Cloud' has a simple, uplifting message. What is it?

Clouds get lonely too.

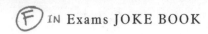

Explore the significance of trust in *Animal Farm*.

Never trust a communist.

Which word is so long there's a mile between the first and last letters?

Smiles!

Which group of fictional characters in the Harry Potter series of novels are led by Lord Voldemort?

The Fellowship.

Summarise *Pride and Prejudice* in one sentence.

Lots of misunderstandings
followed by a marriage.

What are the advantages of using a first-person viewpoint when writing a novel?

You only have to worry about one character.

Charles Dickens' *A Christmas Carol* is a story of hope and redemption. Discuss.

Kermit hopes his son will get better, and he does.

> **TEACHER:** Now, can anyone tell me how many seconds there are in a year?
>
> **PUPIL:** Twelve, Miss – 2nd of January, 2nd of February and one in each of the other months.

Why do athletes breathe faster when sprinting?

Because air is rushing into their mouths.

What runs around a playground but doesn't move?

A fence.

Explain how dehydration affects performance.

Your mouth goes dry and
you can't sing any more

Why does Lycra clothing help a cyclist go faster?

Because they don't want to be
spotted by their friends - the
embarrassment fuels their legs.

In tennis, what does the term 'double fault' mean?

When people start playing a doubles match by accident.

Why was coffee once a banned substance at the Olympic Games?

Everyone was really hyper and annoying.

What is a triathlete?

Someone trying to be an athlete

What is the difference between aerobic and anaerobic exercise?

You do this one
      without breathing.

The decathlon consists of ten track and field events, including throwing a discus. Name one other event.

field - sheep herding.

Why was Dracula sent home from school?

Because of his constant coffin.

What kind of food do arithmetic teachers eat?

Square meals.

What are the psychological benefits of exercise?

If you run lots you're too tired to get psycho.

Explain the term 'oxygen debt'.

Owing a lot to the oxygen bank.

What do the five Olympic rings represent?

The circles on the Olympic coffee table from the athlete's mugs.

What are endorphins?

A type of porpoise

TEACHER: Why were you absent yesterday?

PUPIL: I swallowed some wool, Sir.

TEACHER: Do you think I believe that yarn?

What is considered a normal resting heart rate?

Bu-dum... bu-dum... bu-dum...

How do you make a sausage roll?

Push it down a hill!

What skill is required by gymnasts?

You need to look good in a leotard.

What is the best food for a marathon runner to eat prior to a race?

Fast food to help them go fast.

What is a carnivore?

A person or animal that doesn't like vegetables and greens.

In human digestion, how does food move through the oesophagus?

It slides.

Biology

Where would you find mitochondria?

It's the less serious version of hypochondria, you only think you *might* have something.

How do scientists keep their breath fresh?

With experi-mints.

TEACHER: When was Rome built?

PUPIL: At night, Miss.

TEACHER: Why do you say that?

PUPIL: Because my grandfather always says that Rome wasn't built in a day.

Chlorophyll is a green pigment found in algae and plants. What does it do?

Makes green vegetables taste yucky.

Biology

Give three reasons why young children breathe faster than adults.

1. Because they run around more.
2. They're often overexcited.
3. They only have little lungs.

What is the main constituent of the human brain?

Grey squishy stuff.

Name one common cause of food poisoning.

poison in food.

Why do magicians excel at school?

They're really good at trick questions.

Give one theory for how migratory birds navigate.

The bird at the front has a compass.

What is a ruminant?

Something that's left over

Birds of paradise are some of the most colourful birds on earth. Give an explanation for their bright plumage.

God liked them more than sparrows.

Which school do door-makers go to?

The school of hard knocks.

What is the world's largest amphibian?

Godzilla

Who was the most famous king to use fractions?

Henry the Eighths.

Name two symptoms of food poisoning.

My dad and brother doing a bbq.

Biology

Why do humans shrink in size as they grow older?

So they can fit into retirement homes.

What was Darwin's theory of evolution?

See no evil, hear no evil, do no evil.

Why do we need carbohydrates in our diet?

So we don't become carbodehydrated.

Chemistry

Atoms are made up of protons, neutrons and ....

Megatron.

What is the process that causes a substance to change from a solid to a liquid?

Diarrhoea.

Why are school catering staff
so cruel?

Because they batter fish, beat eggs and
whip cream.

Name one natural source of radiation.

Radiators.

Twenty per cent of the earth's oxygen is produced by
which ecosystem?

Air - conditioning.

The alloy nitinol is a smart material made from nickel and titanium. What is a 'smart material'?

Things they use for phones.

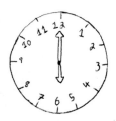

Why was the clock given detention?

For tocking in class!

Why might it be dangerous to bury radioactive waste underground?

You don't want to mess
with the moles.

Why is it impossible for oil and water to mix together?

They're in different
social classes.

The race is on to find an efficient alternative energy before the earth runs out of fossil fuel. Name two potential renewable sources of energy.

Rechargeable batteries.
Human methane.

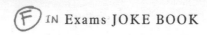

What is the most abundant element in the universe?

Gas.

What is a quark?

The sound a poorly duck makes.

A 'pH' scale is a measure of what?

Personal hygiene.

Give a brief explanation of the meaning of the term 'absolute zero'.

You are a nerd and no one likes you.

LUCY: *How do we know that the Egyptians invented tennis?*

LOUISE: *I don't know.*

LUCY: *Because, in the Bible, it says that Joseph served in Pharaoh's court.*

What kind of tool do you need for arithmetic?

A pair of multi-pliers!

What is the role of a catalyst in a chemical reaction?

It lists the cats involved.

Nylon and polyester are examples of what?

Tights.

Which substance expands as it freezes?

Satan's privates.

What do you call a teacher who has lost their students?

Happy.

Give two weather conditions associated with high pressure.

Sweat and a hot head.

How can you reduce your risk of being struck by lightning?

Crawl.

Geography

What is a cyclone?

A setting on a washing machine.

Where is the hottest place on earth?

A sauna.

What goes around the world but stays in one corner?

A stamp.

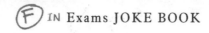

Why do earthquakes and volcanoes often occur in the same areas?

Bad luck.

What are sinkholes and what is thought to cause them?

We use them to get waste water to the drains.

What is a runner's favourite subject?

Jog-raphy!

Geography

What is the ozone layer and why is it vital to life on earth?

It's the bubble round the earth that stops the space getting in.

What are the implications of Arctic warming?

All the arctic rolls will melt.

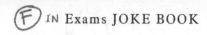

What are the properties of clay soil?

Clay and soil.

What is deforestation?

Removal of pubic hair.

Define the phrase 'population density'.

Who is clever and who is stupid in the population.

What is a butterfly's favourite subject at school?

Mothmatics.

Name two animals native to Australia.

Two dingoes.

What is crop rotation?

Spinning a single carrot
by its leaves.

What problems do countries with high population-growth rates face?

They have to change the height of
all the doors so the
population will fit through.

Geography

Over the past few years there has been a significant decline in honeybees. Suggest one reason for this.

No one likes honey any more.

Which word begins and ends with an 'e' but only contains one letter?

An envelope.

Psychology

What are the three levels or parts of the mind, according to Sigmund Freud?

Willies, bottoms + boobies.

According to Sigmund Freud, what are the id, the ego and the superego?

Types of action hero.

Psychology

What does CBT stand for?

Constant Brain Tension.

Why do witches love going to English class?

Because they're good at spell-ings!

Why did the girl do her maths classwork on the floor?

Because the teacher told her to do it without using tables.

Give two symptoms of depression.

Being dented and bent in.

Psychology

In counselling, what does 'setting boundaries' mean?

Building yourself
a little wall.

How many hemispheres are there in the brain?

The southern and the northern.

Suggest a physical technique for managing stress.

Hitting something.

There are five different types of electrical patterns in the brain. Delta waves, for example, are dominant during deep sleep. Name one other brainwave and state when it occurs.

Tidal waves when you dream about the sea.

The formula for water is H_2O. What is the formula for ice?

H_2O cubed.

We breathe oxygen during the day.
What do we breathe at night?

Nitrogen.

Give an example of 'learned helplessness'.

When you don't know what
the teacher's talking about.

Why are our memories often unreliable?

Because they're fuzzy and vague.

Name two common phobias.

Work.
School.

What is a Rorschach inkblot test and what is it used for?

Testing ink pens.

What is psychological 'projection'?

Watching Psycho at the cinema.

What did the ink pen say to
the pencil?

What's your point?

What is the hormone that is released when we hug or
kiss a loved one?

Passion.

```
┌─────────────────────────┐
│                         │
│        I.T.             │
│   _____   │
│                         │
└─────────────────────────┘
```

What is a firewall?

A wall of fire.

What is a vlog?

A sort of Russian clog.

What is a math teacher's favourite dessert?

Pi.

When shopping online, what symbol should you look out for in the bottom right of the browser window to ensure the site is secure?

The 'on' button.

What is a hyperlink?

Any link that leads to websites selling coffee or drugs.

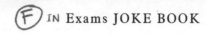

Name two different operating systems.

Keyhole surgery and just normal
cutting someone up.

What does the term URL stand for?

Ugly Rejected Lovers.

Name two things you would plug into a USB port.

A plug, then another plug.

Why are increasing numbers of people using stand-up work stations?

Because their chairs keep breaking.

Why is the sun the happiest thing in the sky?

Because it's always beaming!

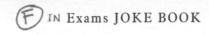

What is a USB port used for?

USB ships

What are the benefits of using a tablet PC over a desktop?

You don't need to get out of bed.

When composing an email, why might you use the BCC (blind carbon copy) function?

For the visually impaired.

It's sort of like electronic Braille.

Why was the ghost of Anne Boleyn always running after the ghost of Henry VIII?

She was trying to get ahead!

If a document is encrypted, what does this mean?

It's written in hieroglyphics.

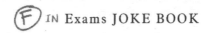

Why do bees have sticky hair?

Because of the honeycombs!

What is an appropriate way of ensuring your data is automatically backed up every day?

Text it to someone.

I.T.

When would you use a scatter chart?

To log loose bowel movements.

What is a binary number?

Any number with a two in it.

What did Noah do to pass time on the ark?

He fished, but he didn't catch much because he only had two worms.

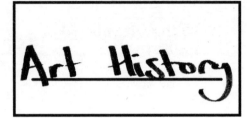

Why are Monet's water lilies so popular?

They're easy to grow and look pretty in your pond.

Where would you find the Acropolis?

Krypton.

How were the Vikings able to send covert messages?

By Norse code.

Define the term 'iconoclasm'.

When celebrities have no class.

In 1917 an artist submitted a porcelain urinal as a sculpture to an exhibition in New York City and signed it 'R. Mutt'. What was the artist's real name?

Robert Dog.

Tempera is a fast-drying painting medium which is made by mixing coloured pigment with which glutinous substance?

Batter, and frying it.

Why is remembering your English history like a classroom?

Too many rulers!

Art History

What is a triptych?

When you've taken lots of drugs and it's still having effects

Name three visual art forms.

Short-distance, mid-range and long-distance viewing.

Name two pioneers of abstract art.

Jackson Bollock

Boris Johnson

What is the difference between modern and postmodern architecture?

Post.

Christopher Wren designed which famous landmark in London?

The Millenium Bridge.

Why was Rodin's first public sculpture – *The Vanquished* – initially so unpopular with the general public?

They weren't comfortable with public art yet.

Art History

Throughout history, art has been placed in outdoor spaces for the enjoyment of the public. Give one modern example and explain how the work's placement conveys meaning to its audience.

Art that's been left outside usually means it's a bit rubbish and no one wants it any more.

Which musical instrument do fishermen play?

The castanet.

The entrance to the Louvre Museum in Paris is famous for what reason?

It opens the doors to the Mona Lisa.

What French phrase is used to describe artists or ideas that are ahead of their time?

C'est bizarre!

Why did the music teacher bring a ladder into class?

So he could reach the high notes!

> **Which English king invented the fireplace?**
>
> *Alfred the Grate!*

What are the key characteristics of Gothic art?

Loads of black and loads of eyeliner.

Photography

What does SLR mean?

Single Line Railway.

Why is reportage photography often used for weddings?

Everyone likes to have their photo in the paper.

What did the triangle say to the circle?

You're pointless!

What is red eye and how can you prevent it?

The quick plane frome California to New York. You can prevent it by causing a panic at the airport gates so they can't take off.

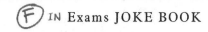
Name two lights commonly used in portrait photography.

Ceiling lights and lamps,
depending on what's in the room.

What type of music are balloons afraid of?

Pop music!

Photography

In portraiture, why might you place a white umbrella close to a subject?

In case it starts raining.

What is a photo filter?

One of the stages on Instagram

What's the best shutter speed for shooting high-speed action?

High speed.

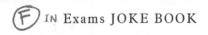

When would you use a JPEG compression?

If not everyone could fit in the picture.

Ansel Adams is best known which type of photography?

Goth family portraits.

Give one positive and one negative impact of digital photography on the environment.

Fewer photos in the rubbish is a good thing but more people are taking rubbish photos of nature.

Photography

Discuss how digital photography has affected social aspects of our culture.

It has made Kim Kardashian's bottom famous.

Why did the cyclops have to close his school?

Because he only had one pupil.

How many pixels are in a megapixel?

One really big one.

Image resolution is measured in PPI. What does PPI stand for?

Payment Protechon Insurance

State one disadvantage of having a high ISO setting.

When you forget to switch to a low ISO setting.

Did you hear about the two friends playing football with peas in a saucer?

They were playing for the cup.

Why couldn't the music teacher get into her classroom?

Her keys were on the piano.

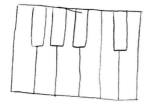

When would you use a telephoto lens?

When you're taking a photo of a TV.

Why is sound such a powerful film technique?

Because silent movies are so 1920s.

In film editing, what is fade in/fade out?

It's to do with the fashion in denim jeans worn in the film.

What is the function of continuity in TV and film?

It allows you to keep watching Netflix for hours without having to move.

Why do fluorescent lights always hum?

Because they can't remember the words!

The media industry is 'self-regulated'. What does this mean?

It controls its own alcohol intake.

Why is the school football pitch always wet?

Because the players can't stop dribbling.

Why do Religious Studies teachers eat Swiss cheese?

Because it's hole-y!

What is a broadsheet newspaper?

The opposite of narrowsheet papers.

What is a tabloid newspaper?

A newspape that
keeps tabs on everything.

What are the main advantages of a music magazine being available on the internet?

There aren't any because you can't
read the magazine and listen to
You Tube clips at the same time.

What is copyright and how long does it last?

A law that lasts as long as the copy is right.

Why are 'niche' audiences important for media producers?

Because dots of audiences watch films in alcoves.

How did the school cook propose
to his girlfriend?

With an onion ring.

Give two examples of products aimed at a 'niche' audience.

Small sofas or armchairs.

What is an indie author?

An author who is into indie music.

Why are e-books becoming increasingly popular?

Because any word with an 'e' in prank of it looks cool.

THIS WAY UP

Why are artist websites important to the music industry?

Because painters like to listen to music when they're painting

What is a retweet?

Singing back a bird's call.

Why do you think television drama is so popular with television audiences?

Because documentaries can be boring.

Which Shakespearean play do baby pigs read?

Hamlet.

What is a non-custodial sentence?

Being sentenced to eat desserts without custard.

Explain the role of a youth offending team.

They go around insulting teenagers.

What is meant by 'cultural identity'?

Your passport.

Why is Shakespeare like a
harsh judge?

Both of them use difficult sentences.

State one reason why countries elect to be part of international organisations such as the United Nations and the European Union.

So they can take part in the Eurovision.

What is the most mathematical part of speech?

The 'add verb'.

What is the International Monetary Fund (IMF)?

Money that anyone can have when
they need it, although I haven't
seen any g it.

State one reason why people might choose to migrate
to a different country.

Because of the rain.

What is the role of the Commonwealth?

It makes sure the wealthy people are commoners.

How does a parliament help citizens get their voices heard?

Free elocution classes.

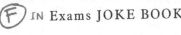

What is a pressure group?

When your mates make you
smoke fags.

What's the difference between the High Court and
Supreme Court?

The High Court evolves into the Supreme Court
like a Pokémon.

> **Ten cats are sitting on a fence. If one jumps off, how many are left?**
>
> None, they were all copycats!

Explain why people join political parties.

For the buffet food and free drinks.

Explain the role of a prime minister.

Ham salad.

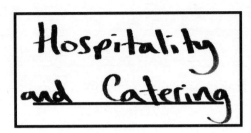

Hospitality and Catering

What is meant by the term 'convenience food'?

Food that is close to hand.

Why are convenience foods becoming more popular?

Well, no one likes an inconvenience food.

What three letters make a musical instrument?

P-N-O.

Why is it important to read food labels carefully?

In case you have won a prize.

Define 'hidden sugars'.

The packets at the back of the cupboard behind the flour.

Why don't chickens like playing football?

They keep being sent off for fowl play.

112

What advice would you give someone who wanted to cut back on their hidden sugar intake?

Eat fun-size bars

Pasta is an example of a carbohydrate. Give two other examples.

Spaghetti and linguine.

Name three different ways in which food can be cooked.

Rare, medium, well-cooked.

Why do some people prefer to steam their vegetables?

We are all different.

Why are preservatives added to food products?

Mind control.

Give two reasons why someone might prefer to eat home-baked bread over shop-bought bread.

1. They're poor.
2. Agoraphobia.

Why was Cinderella kicked off the school hockey team?

She kept running away from the ball.

What does 'home preservation' refer to? Give one example.

Preserving your home
eg. not kicking holes
through walls.

Which athlete is the most good-looking?

A sprinter, because he's always dashing.

Why is an increased intake of folic acid recommended during pregnancy?

It stops hiccups, so you don't wet yourself.

What does it mean if you are lactose intolerant?

You're really mean to lactose.

Name two factors which influence an individual's daily energy requirements.

1. How lazy they are.

2. What's in the pridge.

Why are nutrients added to white flour by law?

Secret goverment plot to fatten us all up.

Why do golfers wear two pairs of pants?

In case they get a hole in one!

Design and
Technology

What is market pull?

The opposite of a market push.

What is technology push?

Push notifications like when Twitter
pops up on your phone.

What has a bed but never sleeps?

A river.

Give two examples of obsolete technologies.

Dino-calculator and i-Dodo.

Design and Technology

What does 'planned obsolescence' refer to and why might it be harmful to the environment?

Fast food companies making teenagers fat on purpose.

Increased methane emissions.

What steps might a manufacturer take in order to protect their invention from being copied?

Never showing it to anyone.

Why are production lines used in commercial manufacturing?

Production circles don't go anywhere.

LUCY: I don't think I'll bother coming back to school.

LOUISE: Why ever not?

LUCY: Our teachers aren't up to very much – all they do is ask *us* questions!

Design and Technology

State two renewable materials.

1. Wee.
2. Poo.

How has flat-pack furniture changed the way people furnish their homes?

They now furnish their homes while swearing more.

Why did Dracula give up on art class?

Because he could only draw blood.

State one advantage of Computer Aided Manufacture (CAM).

Computers don't get their hands mangled.

Design and Technology

Describe how a designer might use a computer in the development of a new table lamp.

They might google 'table lamp design'

If a hairdryer is designed ergonomically, what does this mean?

It's sort of like astronomically but cheaper.

What's a librarian's favourite vegetable?

Quiet peas.

When designing packaging for a product, name three factors that need to be considered.

1. How long it will take.
2. Can corners be cut?
3. What time you're having lunch.

What is brand identity?

When you namecheck designer labels in your Twitter bio.

Design and Technology

Why are librarians lonely?

They are always working by them shelves.

Why is brand identity important?

Shows you've got lots of money.

How are anthropometrics used in product design?

Monkeys are used to test how sturdy the product is.

If you're interested in finding out more
about our books, find us on Facebook at
Summersdale Publishers
and follow us on Twitter at @Summersdale.

www.summersdale.com